DOWN ON THE FUNNY FARM WITH COW AND FRIENDS

DOWN ON THE FUNNY FARM WITH COW AND FRIENDS

A Joke Book from the Barnyard Gang

JB FRANK

Sky Pony Press
New York

Sky Pony Press books may be purchased in bulk at special discounts for sales promotion, corporate gifts, fund-raising, or educational purposes. Special editions can also be created to specifications. For details, contact the Special Sales Department, Sky Pony Press, 307 West 36th Street, 11th Floor, New York, NY 10018 or info@skyhorsepublishing.com.

Sky Pony® is a registered trademark of Skyhorse Publishing, Inc.®, a Delaware corporation.

Visit our website at www.skyponypress.com.

10 9 8 7 6 5 4 3 2

Manufactured in the United States of America, 2025
This product conforms to CPSIA 2008

Library of Congress Cataloging-in-Publication Data is available on file.

Cover design by Kai Texel
Cover images from Shutterstock

Print ISBN: 978-1-5107-8128-3
Ebook ISBN: 978-1-5107-8129-0

Dedication

To my sisters and brothers: Mary, Catherine, Peter, Lucille, Joseph, Celeste, Rita, John, Thomas, Dolores, Margaret, Daniel, and Carol

“Hi. My name is Cow. I love telling jokes. I have a really good one to tell you.”

Wait! Jokes are my favorite things.

Okay, here's the joke. What did—

I've got some that are so funny you'll laugh until snot comes out of your nose.

Okay, go ahead, but some of your jokes are a little gross.

What's invisible and smells like hay?

I'm udder-ly clueless.

A horse fart!

Pee-ew, Horse! Snot funny. Now, my turn—

And I've got more!

Okay, let 'em rip!

Q: Why do cowboys like to ride horses?

A: Because horses are too heavy to carry.

Q: How many horses does it take to pull Farmer John's wagon?

A: None—he got a pickup truck instead.

Q: What disease was the horse scared of getting?

A: Hay fever!

Q: How long should a horse's legs be?
A: Long enough to reach the ground.

Q: Which side of the horse has the most hair?
A: The outside!

Q: Why did the man stand behind the horse?
A: He was hoping to get a kick out of it.

Q: Which kind of horse likes to eat baked beans?

A: The pinto.*

Q: What's the difference between a horse and a duck?

A: One goes quick, and the other goes quack.

Q: What's a vampire's favorite part of a horse race?

A: When it's neck and neck.

Q: What did the horse say when it fell?

A: "I've fallen, and I can't giddy up!"

Q: What did the teacher say when the horse walked into the class?

A: "Why the long face?"

Q: What kind of horse can jump higher than a house?

A: All of them! Houses can't jump at all.

Q: Where do horses shop for clothes?
A: At Old Neigh-vy.

Q: How do you know when a horse has a negative attitude?
A: He says neigh to everything.

Q: What did the lunch lady say to the horses?
A: "Stop horsing around."

Q: What do you call a witch horse?
A: A nightmare.

Q: Where do racehorses eat?
A: At fast food restaurants.

Q: What did the waiter say to the horse?
A: "Can I get you a stable?"

Q: What does it mean when you find a horseshoe?

A: A horse is walking around barefoot.

Q: What's the hardest thing about riding a horse?

A: The ground.

Q: What do you call a pony that has a sore throat?

A: A little hoarse.

Q: Have you heard the one about the runaway horse?

A: It's a terrible tale of WHOA!

Q: What happened when the horse swallowed four quarters?

A: It bucked.

Q: What did the horse grow in her garden?

A: Horse radishes.

Q: What kind of stories do depressed horses tell?

A: Tails of whoa.

Q: What do you call a well-balanced horse?

A: Stable.

Q: Why did the horse talk with his mouth full?

A: He had bad stable manners.

Q: What do you call a horse that can't lose a race?

A: Sherbet.

Q: Why was the racehorse named Bad News?

A: Everyone knows that bad news travels fast.

Q: What's black and white and eats like a horse?

A: A zebra.

Q: What kind of horse swims underwater without having to come up for air?

A: A seahorse.

You heard them straight from the horse's mouth! I don't horse around when it comes to telling jokes.

Jokes! I love jokes. I don't always tell them well, but I love jokes.

Hello, Squirrel. I was just going to tell a joke.

Wait! I do have one joke that will drive you nuts.

I like nutty jokes.

When does a squirrel take a bath?

Do you take baths?

Rolls eyes It's a joke, Cow.

Oh, of course. Sorry. No clue.

When no one's looking.

I don't get it.

Now it's my turn.

First me! My jokes are so baaaad, they're really good.

Let's hear these baaaad jokes!

Q: What did the kid want so he would look hip?

A: A goatee.

Q: Why was the goat so embarrassed?

A: She saw the ranch dressing.

Q: What do they call a goat with one horn?

A: A unicorn.

Q: Where do goats buy their office supplies?
A: Stables.

Q: What did the goat say after drinking spoiled milk?
A: "This tastes so baaaaaad."

Q: Why are French goats better musicians than other goats?
A: They're born with French horns.

Q: What do you get when you cross an angry goat with a grumpy cow?

A: An animal that's in a baaaaaaad moooooood.

Q: What do you call a mountain goat?

A: A hillbilly.

Q: Why do the goats avoid the cows in the barn?

A: The cows are too mooo-dy.

Q: What is as big as a goat but weighs nothing?

A: His shadow.

Q: What time is it when a billy goat nibbles your hat?

A: Time to get a new hat!

Q: What did the goat say to the cow?

A: "I've got no beef with you."

Q: Why did the goat wear a bell around his neck?

A: Because his horn didn't work.

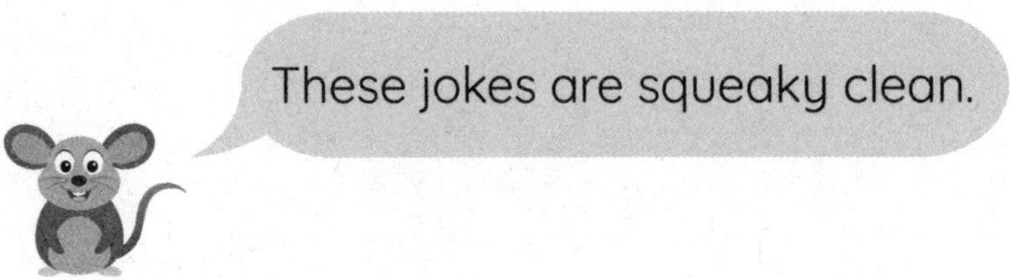

Q: Why was the barn so noisy?

A: Because all of the goats had horns.

Q: What do you get when you cross a Smurf with a goat?

A: Blue cheese!

Q: What do you get when you cross an octopus and a goat?

A: An animal that can milk itself.

Q: What do you get when you cross an owl with a goat?

A: A hootenanny!

Q: Why was the goat farmer so wealthy?

A: He had a lot of bucks!

Q: What do grumpy goats say during the holidays?

A: "Baaaaa humbug."

Q: What do you call it when a nanny goat falls off a cliff?

A: An udder catastrophe.

Q: Why was the soccer-playing goat the most valuable player?

A: He was the G.O.A.T.*

Q: Why don't nanny goats remember things you tell them?

A: Because everything goes in one ear and out the udder.

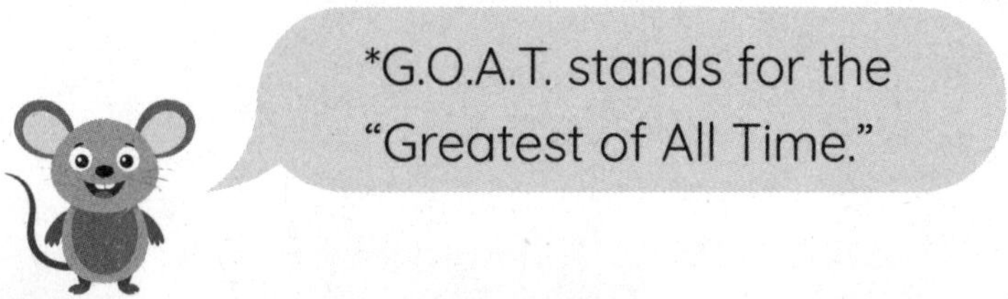

Q: What did the kid goat want to be when she grew up?

A: A baaa-llerina.

Q: How did the goat label its belongings?

A: With a permanent markhor.*

Q: Where do goats get haircuts?

A: At the baa-baa shop!

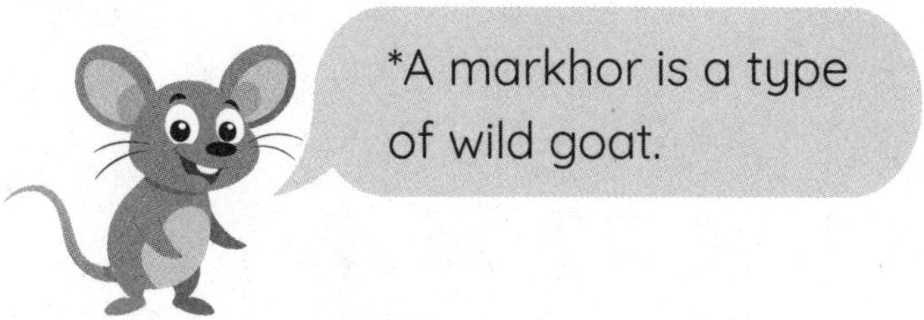

Q: What did the nanny goat serve for breakfast?

A: Goat-meal.

Q: What do you call an extremely lazy goat that just stands around?

A: Billy Idol.

What barks and has feathers?

What?

A bird dog.

The jokes are supposed to be about goats.

Q: What did everyone call the goat that sailed around the world?

A: Billy Ocean.

Q: Why did the goat run straight into a wall?

A: He didn't see the ewe turn.

Q: Why is it so hard to have a conversation with a goat?

A: Because they keep butting in.

Q: How do you prevent a goat from charging?
A: Take away his credit card.

Q: Did you hear about the goat that knew kung fu?
A: He was a karate kid.

Funny how goats can be part of a trip without going anywhere. (A group of goats is called "a trip.")

Two goats are eating garbage. The first goat finds a roll of film and eats it. When he has finished it, the second goat asks him, “How did you like the movie?” The first goat responds, “It was OK, but I liked the book better.”

Good one, Squirrel. You goat me!

I think goats have the best jokes.
No kidding.

Here comes Pig!
We're telling jokes, Pig.

These will surely make
you squeal!

Q: Why did the pig dump her boyfriend?

A: Because he was a real boar.

Q: Which *Star Wars* character was really a pig?

A: Ham Solo.

Q: What do piglets do after school?

A: Their ham-work!

Q: What do you call it when you cross a dinosaur with a pig?

A: Jurassic pork!

Q: What's the difference between bird flu and swine flu?

A: You need tweet-ment for the bird flu, but you need oink-ment for the swine flu.

Q: What happened when the pigpen broke?

A: They switched to a pencil.

What's the difference between
a filing cabinet and a pig?

I don't know.

Well, then I certainly won't let you
file any of my papers.

You don't have papers.

It's a joke.

Oh, right. Mooo mistake.

Q: Which sport was invented by pigs?
A: Mud wrestling.

Q: What do pigs dress as on Halloween?
A: Frankenswine.

Q: What do you get when you cross a pig with a scary dinosaur?
A: A pork-asaurus rex!

Q: What did the pig say when the wolf grabbed his tail?

A: "That's the end of me!"

Q: What do pigs do on sunny days?

A: They go on pig-nics.

Q: How do pigs greet their parents?

A: With hogs and kisses!

Q: What's another name for the story *The Three Little Pigs?*

A: *A Pig Tale!*

Q: What do you call a fake pig story?

A: A lot of hogwash.

Q: Who is the greatest pig painter?

A: Pigcasso.

Q: What do pig sailors yell when they stop their ships?

A: Oinkers aweigh!

Q: What do you call a pig that drives all over the road?

A: A road hog.

Q: Who rolls around in the mud and delivers cute baskets?

A: The Easter Piggy.

Q: How did the farmer know the goat was stealing eggs?

A: The pigs squealed on him.

Q: What do you call a pig thief?

A: A ham-burglar.

Q: What do you call it when you're walking around and a group of pigs jumps out of a tree at you?

A: It's a ham-bush.

Q: What kind of parties do pigs like to throw?
A: Sow-prize parties!

Q: Why should you never tell a pig a secret?
A: They love to squeal.

Q: Which actor do pigs like the least?
A: Kevin Bacon.

Q: What do you get when you cross a pig and a cactus?

A: A porky-pine.

Q: Why should you never share a bed with a pig?

A: They always hog the covers.

Q: What do you call a pig that does karate?

A: A pork chop.

Q: Why did the pig lose the race?
A: He pulled a hamstring.

Q: Why are pig books so interesting?
A: There's always a twist in the tale.

Q: Where do pigs keep their money?
A: Why in the piggy bank, of course.

Farmer Giles is so interested in conserving energy, he built a pig-powered car. He has to get rid of it, though. Every time he turns a corner, the tires squeal.

I want to jump in! Why are frogs so happy?

I don't know.

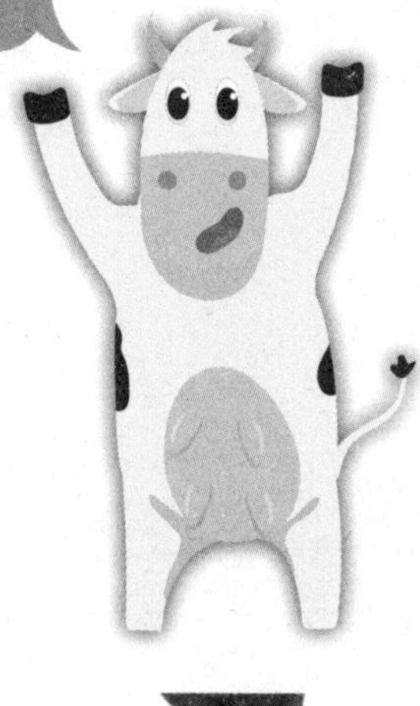

Because we eat what bugs us.

CORNY!

I have another joke that will really croak you up. What happens to a frog's car when his meter runs out?

Wha-a-a-t??

It gets toad! Get it? TOAD!

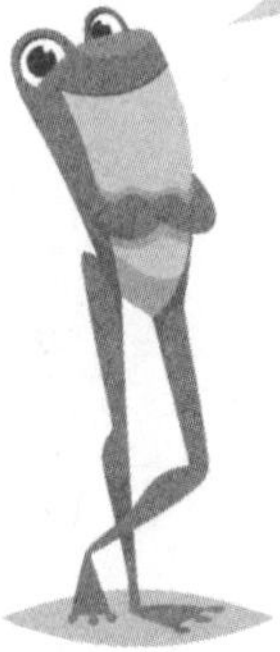

Lame.

I can't believe I haven't told you my joke yet.

I've got a quick one. Cow, what do you get when you cross a cow with a duck?

I give up.

Milk and quackers!

Let’s not hog all the good jokes. Here comes Chicken.

I have a few egg-stra special jokes to tell.

Q: How do monsters like their eggs?
A: Terri-fried.

Q: Why do hens lay eggs?
A: Because they'd break if they dropped them.

Q: Why did the cactus cross the road?
A: It was stuck to the chicken.

Q: Why did the toad hop across the road?
A: He was following the chicken.

Q: Why did the chicken join a band?
A: Because it already had the drumsticks.

Q: What do you call a crazy chicken?
A: A cuckoo cluck.

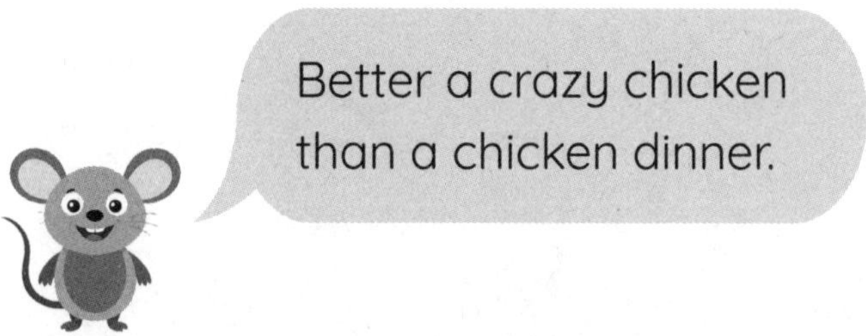

Knock, knock.

Who's there?

Tank.

Tank who?

You're welcome.

Q: Why did the rooster run away?
A: He was chicken.

Q: Why did the chicken cross the basketball court?
A: He heard the referee calling fowls.

Q: What do bad chickens lay?
A: Deviled eggs.

Q: Why did the sheep cross the road?

A: Because the chicken needed a day off.

Q: What do you call a rooster who wakes you up every morning?

A: An alarm cluck.

Q: Why did the baby chick cross the road?

A: It was "take your child to work" day.

Q: If the rooster laid an egg on a roof, which way would the egg roll?

A: Neither way! Roosters don't lay eggs.

Q: Which dance will a chicken never do?

A: The foxtrot.

Q: What happened to the chicken who found a four-leaf clover?

A: He had good cluck forever.

Q: How do baby chickens dance?

A: Chick to chick (cheek to cheek).

Q: Since chickens rise when the rooster crows, when do ducks wake up?

A: At the quack of dawn.

Q: What do you get when you cross a hen with a dog?

A: Pooched eggs.

Q: How do chickens bake cakes?

A: From scratch.

Q: What do you call it when it rains chickens and ducks?

A: Fowl weather.

Q: When is chicken soup not good for your health?

A: When you're the chicken.

Q: What did the chicken say when it laid a square egg?

A: "Ouch!"

Q: Which holy man do chickens dread most?

A: A friar.

Q: What happened when the hen ate cement?

A: She laid a sidewalk.

Q: What do all the hens do on a Saturday night?

A: Watch a chick flick.

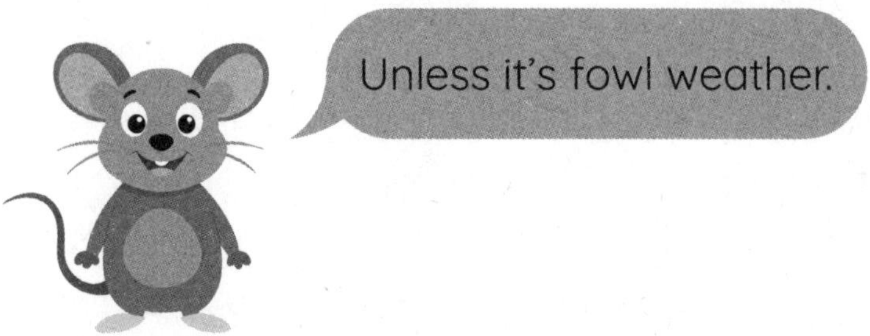

Q: How did the egg climb the hill?

A: It scrambled up.

Q: What do you call a bird that's scared of flying?

A: A chicken.

Q: Why didn't the chicken skeleton cross the road?

A: He didn't have the guts.

Q: If fruit comes from a fruit tree, where would a chicken come from?

A: A poul-tree.

Q: What do you get when you cross a chicken and a centipede?

A: Drumsticks for everyone!

My jokes were eggs-traordinarily funny. I hope you agree.

Well, you've heard from Horse, Squirrel, Goat, Pig, Frog, Duck, and Chicken. Now you get to hear my jokes!

Cow, sorry we hogged all the time!

Mooove over. Here come the funny jokes!

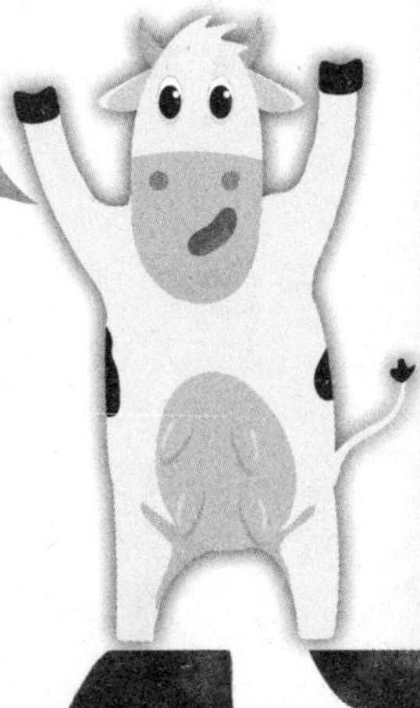

Q: Why won't cows join the police force?

A: They refuse to participate in steak-outs.

Q: What do you call a rude cow?

A: Beef jerky.

Q: Why couldn't the two cows get along?

A: Because they had beef with one another.

Q: What do you call a cow with no legs?

A: Ground beef.

Q: What do you call a sleeping bull?

A: A bulldozer.

Q: Why do cows have hooves instead of feet?

A: Because they lactose.

Q: What do you call a group of cows with a sense of humor?

A: A laughing stock.

Q: What do you call a cow with no calf?

A: Decaffeinated.

Q: Why did the cow want to get in the rocket ship?

A: He wanted to go to udder space!

Q: What do you call a cow who just hit the lottery?

A: A cash cow.

Q: What do you get when a cow jumps on a trampoline?

A: A milkshake!

Q: Where do cows go on Friday nights?

A: To the mooovies.

Q: What did the cow say to the boy sitting in his chair?

A: "Mooove."

Q: Why did the farmer want brown cows?

A: Because he wanted chocolate milk.

Q: What is a cow's favorite type of play?

A: A moo-sical!

Q: What did one dairy cow say to the other?
A: "Got milk?"

Q: What do you call a cow that doesn't give milk?
A: A Milk Dud.

"Knock, knock!"
"Who's there?"
"Cows go."
"Cows go who?"
"No, silly! Cows go moo."

Q: What do you use to count cows?

A: A cow-culator.

Q: What would you call a cow wearing armor?

A: Sir Loin.

Q: How did the farmer find his lost cow?

A: He tractor down!

Q: How do cows introduce their wives?
A: "Hey, guys! Meat Patty."

Q: What did the cow say when someone told her a lie?
A: "Sounds like a lot of bull to me."

Q: What do you call a cow on a diet?
A: Lean beef.

Q: How do you make Swiss cheese?

A: With milk from a holey cow.

Q: What did the cow shout when it did a cannonball into the swimming pool?

A: "Cow-abunga!"

Q: Why is it so hard to hurt a cow's feelings?

A: Their hides are thick.

Q: Why did the cow cross the road?
A: To get to the udder side.

Q: What animal goes, "Oom, oom"?
A: A cow walking backwards.

Q: What did the cow say when the farmer pulled its tail?
A: "How dairy!"

Q: How do you get a cow to be quiet?
A: You press the mooot button.

Q: Why does a milking stool have only three legs?
A: The cow has the udder.

What did you think?

There are so many more jokes to tell, but let us know if you liked these and be sure to share your favorites at jbfrankwrites.com!

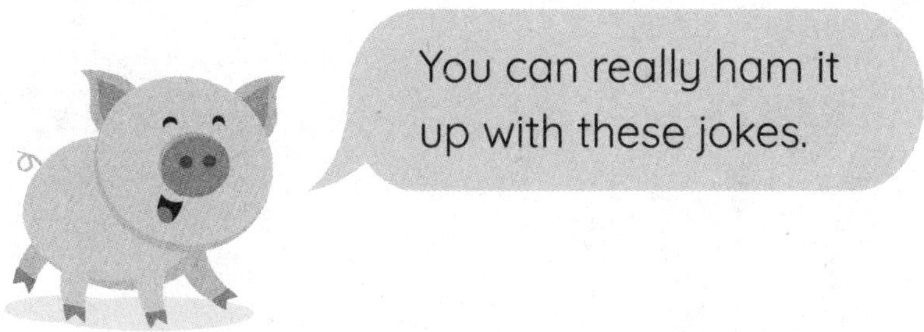

Pony up and tell
us your favorite.

Whatever floats your goat!

It's simply mooo-velous!

Write your own jokes!

Do you like to tell jokes? It's even more fun to make up your own. One element that's in all jokes is the element of surprise! When you surprise your audience, that makes them laugh.

The best way to make up a joke is to think of funny things that have happened to you or to someone else.

Here are a few popular formats that you can use to create your own jokes:

1. **Knock-knock jokes**

   Example: Knock, knock!

   Who's there?

   Rice and beans.

   Rice and beans who?

   Rice and beans, it's morning!

2. **What's the difference between X and Y?**
   Example: What's the difference between a guitar and a fish?
   You can't tuna fish!

3. **What does X have in common with Y?**
   Example: What does cake have in common with baseball?
   They both have batter!

4. **What do you call a . . . ?**
   Example: What do you call a bear with no teeth?
   A gummy bear.

You'll have your family and friends laughing in no time.

When telling a joke, make sure that you present it well. For example, be sure to pause and get everyone's attention. Don't rush through your joke. Speak clearly and loudly enough that everyone can hear you. Pause before delivering the punch line. It helps if you smile when you're done!

And most importantly, have fun! Use the following pages to write down your own jokes.

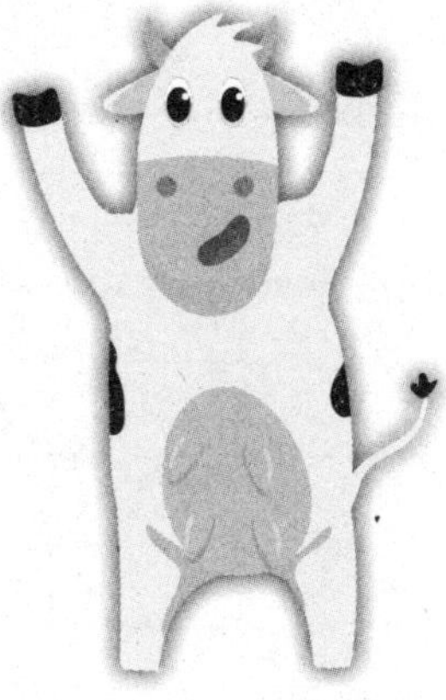